Sadness
And
Happiness

Poems
by
Robert Pinsky

Princeton University Press

Princeton, New Jersey

Copyright © 1975 by Princeton University Press
Published by Princeton University Press
41 William Street, Princeton, New Jersey 08540
In the United Kingdom: Princeton University Press,
Chichester, West Sussex
All Rights Reserved

Library of Congress Cataloging-in-Publication Data

Pinsky, Robert.
Sadness and happiness.

I. Title.
PS3566.I54S2 811'.5'4 75-3486
ISBN 0-691-06295-1

Publication of this book has been aided by the Louis A. Robb Fund
of Princeton University Press
This book has been composed in Linotype Baskerville

http://pup.princeton.edu

Printed in the United States of America

Fifth printing, 1995

10 9 8 7

Designed by Bruce D. Campbell

Contents

I. The Time Of Year, The Time Of Day

Poem About People

The jaunty crop-haired graying
Women in grocery stores,
Their clothes boyish and neat,
New mittens or clean sneakers,

Clean hands, hips not bad still,
Buying ice cream, steaks, soda,
Fresh melons and soap—or the big
Balding young men in work shoes

And green work pants, beer belly
And white T-shirt, the porky walk
Back to the truck, polite; possible
To feel briefly like Jesus,

A gust of diffuse tenderness
Crossing the dark spaces
To where the dry self burrows
Or nests, something that stirs,

Watching the kinds of people
On the street for a while—
But how love falters and flags
When anyone's difficult eyes come

Into focus, terrible gaze of a unique
Soul, its need unlovable: my friend
In his divorced schoolteacher
Apartment, his own unsuspected

Paintings hung everywhere,
Which his wife kept in a closet—
Not, he says, that she wasn't
Perfectly right; or me, mis-hearing

My rock radio sing my self-pity:
"The Angels Wished Him Dead"—all
The hideous, sudden stare of self,
Soul showing through like the lizard

Ancestry showing in the frontal gaze
Of a robin busy on the lawn.
In the movies, when the sensitive
Young Jewish soldier nearly drowns

Trying to rescue the thrashing
Anti-semitic bully, swimming across
The river raked by nazi fire,
The awful part is the part truth:

Hate my whole kind, but me,
Love me for myself. The weather
Changes in the black of night,
And the dream-wind, bowling across

The sopping open spaces
Of roads, golf-courses, parking lots,
Flails a commotion
In the dripping treetops,

Tries a half-rotten shingle
Or a down-hung branch, and we
All dream it, the dark wind crossing
The wide spaces between us.

The Time Of Year, The Time Of Day

One way I need you, the way I come to need
Our custom of speech, or need this other custom
Of speech in lines, is to alleviate
The weather, the time of year, the time of day.

I mean for instance the way the dusk in late
Winter or early spring recalls adolescence:
The pity of my comical unease
And vague depression on the long walk home

From the grim school through washed-out extra daylight
And the yellow light that waited in kitchen windows,
Daydreaming victories on the long parades
Of artificial brick and bare hydrangea.

But how cold in retrospect the afternoon
And evening even in July could seem,
Cold heralding that now those very hours
Are on the way, the very hours which one

Had better use, which may be what it is
About the time of year and the time of day,
Their burden of a promise but a promise
Limited, that sends folk huddling to their bodies

Or kitchens as colonizers of the day
And of the year, rough settlers who throughout
The stunning winter couple in a fury
To fill the brown width of their tillable plains.

Ceremony For Any Beginning

Against weather, and the random
Harpies—mood, circumstance, the laws
Of biography, chance, physics—
The unseasonable soul holds forth,
Eager for form as a renowned
Pedant, the emperor's man of worth,
Hereditary arbiter of manners.

Soul, one's life is one's enemy.
As the small children learn, what happens
Takes over, and what you were goes away.
They learn it in sardonic soft
Comments of the weather, when it sharpens
The hard surfaces of daylight: light
Winds, vague in direction, like blades

Lavishing their brilliant strokes
All over a wrecked house,
The nude wallpaper and the brute
Intelligence of the torn pipes.
Therefore when you marry or build
Pray to be untrue to the plain
Dominance of your own weather, how it keeps

Going even in the woods when not
A soul is there, and how it implies
Always that separate, cold
Splendidness, uncouth and unkind—
On chilly, unclouded mornings,
Torrential sunlight and moist air,
Leafage and solid bark breathing the mist.

Waiting

When the trains go by
The frozen ground shivers
Inwardly like an anvil.

The sky reaches down
Stiffly into the spaces
Among houses and trees.

A wisp of harsh air snakes
Upward between glove
And cuff, quickening

The sense of the life
Elsewhere of things, the things
You touched, maybe, numb

Handle of a rake; stone
Of a peach; soiled
Band-Aid; book, pants

Or shirt that you touched
Once in a store . . . less
The significant fond junk

Of someone's garage, and less
The cinder out of your eye—
Still extant and floating

In Sweden or a bird's crop—
Than the things that you noticed
Or not, watching from a train:

The cold wide river of things,
Going by like the cold
Children who stood by the tracks

Holding for no reason sticks
Or other things, waiting
For no reason for the trains.

December Blues

At the bad time, nothing betrays outwardly the harsh
    findings,
The studies and hospital records. Carols play.

Sitting upright in the transit system, the widowlike women
Wait, hands folded in their laps, as monumental as bread.

In the shopping center lots, lights mounted on cold
    standards
Tower and stir, condensing the blue vapour

Of the stars; between the rows of cars people in coats walk
Bundling packages in their arms or holding the hands of
    children.

Across the highway, where a town thickens by the tracks
With stores open late and creches in front of the churches, .

Even in the bars a businesslike set of the face keeps off
The nostalgic pitfall of the carols, tugging. In bed,

How low and still the people lie, some awake, holding the
    carols
Consciously at bay, Oh Little Town, enveloped in unease.

Discretions Of Alcibiades

First frost is weeks off, but the prudent man
With house-plants on his front porch marks the season
And moves the potted *ficus* back indoors

While windows can be open for a while.
(The plant prefers a gradual transition.)
—The kid who did his homework, washed his face

And never wore tight pants, kept cherry bombs
And nasty photos in his briefcase (think:
A seventh-grader with a briefcase)—Hantman,

In Student Council with his red-hot bag:
His picture of a lady on all fours,
A Great Dane on her back, was not for sale.

And though he may have sold a bomb or two,
And must have set some off, I like to think
He preferred, like Presidents, their deep reserve.

Speaking of gradual transitions, "plant
Prefers" of course is only an expression.
You might say that the plant prefers to die,

Or wishes it were home, in Borneo,
Preferring never to have seen a window.
The stars are similar: "The wheeling Bear,

One white eye on the Pleiads, rolls another
At glowering Orion." Autumn stars.
On this first chilly dusk, a furry bat,

Warm-blooded, dips and flutters in the sky.
(Some constellations might be called, "The Bat.")
The roles are arbitrary too. The man

Who sleeps with Socrates and Leontes' wife,
Who knocks the cocks from his own effigies,
Or not, simply prefers—to use another

Expression—to hide his briefcase in a bomb.
Consider gods and heroes, how they merge:
(I speak as one believing in the gods,

Especially in quick, reflective Hermes,
So sensitive and practical—like a thief,
Or like long-suffering, shrewd Odysseus).

Apollo, sullen and glamorous obverse
Of Hermes, shrouds himself in dark, or shines,
Like bold Achilles in his tent—or out,

As he prefers. All one. Tithonus, too,
And Alcibiades, balling Lady Luck
Until she dried him up. When people say

"How was your summer?" who is there alive
Who wouldn't like to change sides, go to Sparta
Like Alcibiades, cut your hair, live clean . . .

And then knock up the king's wife on the sly.
That's where the inner briefcase is revealed:
He hoped his heir would be the King of Sparta—

More screwing with Fortuna, man with goddess . . .
From a god's point of view, it is perhaps
Disgusting, if exciting in a way,

Like a dog doing a lady from behind.
The sundry dogs from along the road prefer
To conduct ferocious gang-fucks in a field:

Dogs Only, in the end-of summer fest.
But people, on Cape Cod, the Costa Brava,
Borneo, emulate gods and goddesses:

Rubbing their skin with oil, they sun it brown
Until they all are Spaniard, Jew or Greek—
Wear sandals; ply their boat; keep simple house

Cooking red meat or fish on open fires;
Market for salt; and dance to tinkly music.

Tennis

TO HOWARD WILCOX

I. The Service

The nerve to make a high toss and the sense
Of when the ball is there; and then the nerve
To cock your arm back all the way, not rigid

But loose and ready all the way behind
So that the racket nearly or really touches
Your back far down; and all the time to see

The ball, the seams and letters on the ball
As it seems briefly at its highest point
To stop and hover—keeping these in mind,

The swing itself is easy; forgetting cancer,
Or panic learning how to swim or walk,
Forgetting what the score is, names of plants,

And your first piece of ass, you throw the racket
Easily through Brazil, coins, mathematics
And *haute cuisine* to press the ball from over

And a slight slice at two o'clock or less,
Enough to make it loop in accurately
As, like a fish in water flicking itself

Away, your mind takes up the next concern
With the arm, ball, racket still pressing down
And forward and across your obedient body.

13

II. Forehand

Straightforwardness can be a cruel test,
A kind of stagefright threatening on the cold
And level dais, a time of no excuses.

But think about the word *"stroke,"* how it means
What one does to a cat's back, what a brush
Does through a woman's long hair. Think about

The racket pressing, wiping, guiding the ball
As you stay on it, dragging say seven strings
Across the ball, the top edge leading off

To give it topspin. Think about the ball
As a loaf of bread, you hitting every slice.
Pull back the racket well behind you, drop it

And lift it, meeting the ball well out in front
At a point even with your left hip, stroking
To follow through cross-court. The tarnished coin

Of "follow through," the cat, the loaf of bread,
"Keep your eye on the ball," the dull alloy
Of homily, simile and coach's lore

As maddening, and as helpful, as the Fool
Or Æsop's *Fables*, the coinage of advice:
This is the metal that is never spent.

III. Backhand

Here, panic may be a problem; and in the clench
From back to jaw in panic you may come
Too close and struggling strike out with your arm,

Trying to make the arm do everything,
And failing as the legs and trunk resist.
All of your coinages, and your nerve, may fail . . .

14

What you need is the Uroborus, the serpent
Of energy and equilibrium,
Its tail between its jaws, the female circle

Which makes it easy: all is all, the left
Reflects the right, and if you change the grip
To keep your hand and wrist behind the racket

You suddenly find the swing is just the same
As forehand, except you hit it more in front
Because your arm now hangs in front of you

And not behind. You simply change the grip
And with a circular motion from the shoulder,
Hips, ankles, and knees, you sweep the inverted swing.

IV. Strategy

Hit to the weakness. All things being equal
Hit crosscourt rather than down the line, because
If you hit crosscourt back to him, then he

Can only hit back either towards you (crosscourt)
Or parallel to you (down the line), but never
Away from you, the way that you can hit

Away from him if he hits down the line.
Besides, the net is lowest in the middle,
The court itself is longest corner-to-corner,

So that a crosscourt stroke is the most secure,
And that should be your plan, the plan you need
For winning—though only when hitting from the baseline:

From closer up, hit straight ahead, to follow
The ball to net; and from the net hit shrewdly,
To get him into trouble so he will hit

An error, or a cripple you can kill.
If he gets you in trouble, hit a lob,
And make it towering to make it hard

For him to smash from overhead and easy
For you to have the time to range the backcourt,
Bouncing in rhythm like a dog or seal

Ready to catch an object in mid-air
And rocking its head—as with your plan in mind
You arrange yourself to lob it back, and win.

V. Winning

Call questionable balls his way, not yours;
You lose the point but have your concentration,
The grail of self-respect. Wear white. Mind losing.

Walk, never run, between points: it will save
Your breath, and hypnotize him, and he may think
That you are tired, until your terrible

Swift sword amazes him. By understanding
Your body, you will conquer your fatigue.
By understanding your desire to win

And all your other desires, you will conquer
Discouragement. And you will conquer distraction
By understanding the world, and all its parts.

II. Sadness And Happiness

Sadness And Happiness

I

That they have no earthly measure
is well known—the surprise is
how often it becomes impossible
to tell one from the other in memory:

the sadness of past failures, the strangely
happy—doubtless corrupt—
fondling of them. Crude, empty
though the terms are, they do

organize life: sad American
house-hunting couples with kids
and small savings visit Model Homes
each Sunday for years; humble,

they need closet space, closet
space to organize life . . . in older
countries people seem to be happy
with less closet space. Empty space,

I suppose, also explains *post
coitum triste*, a phenomenon
which on reflection I am happy
to find rare in my memory—not,

II

God knows, that sex isn't crucial,
a desire to get more or better
must underlie the "pain" and "bliss"
of sonnets—or is it a need to *do* better:

A girl touched my sleeve, once,
held it, deep-eyed; life too at times
has come up, looked into my face,
My Lord, how like you this? And I?

Always distracted by some secret
movie camera or absurd audience
eager for cliches, *Ivanhoe*, de blues,
Young Man With A Horn, the star

tripping over his lance, quill, phallic
symbol or saxophone—miserable,
these absurd memories of failure
to see anything but oneself,

my pride, my consciousness, my shame, my
sickly haze of Romance—sick too
the root of joy? "Bale" and "bliss" merge
in a Petrarchist grin, that sleeve's burden

III

or chivalric trophy to bear as
emblem or mark of the holy
idiot: know ye, this natural stood
posing amiss while the best prizes

of life bounced off his vague
pate or streamed between his legs—
did Korsh, Old Russia's bedlam-sage,
enjoy having princesses visit his cell?

Would they dote on me as I shake out
a match, my fountain pen in the same
hand, freckling my dim brow with ink?
Into his muttered babble they read tips

on the market, court, marriage—I too
mutter: *Fool, fool!* or *Death!*
or *Joy!* Well, somewhere in the mind's mess
feelings are genuine, someone's

mad voice undistracted, clarity
maybe of motive and precise need
like an enamelled sky, cool
blue of Indian Summer, happiness

IV

like the sex-drowsy saxophones
rolling flatted thirds of the blues
over and over, rocking the dulcet
rhythms of regret, Black music

which tumbles loss over in the mouth
like a moist bone full of marrow;
the converse is a good mood grown
too rich, like dark water steeping

willow-roots in the shade, spotted
with sun and slight odor of dirt
or death, insane quibbles of self-
regard . . . better to mutter *fool*

or feel solaces of unmerited
Grace, like a road of inexplicable
dells, rises and lakes, found
in a flat place of no lakes—or feel

the senses: cheese, bread, tart
apples and wine, broiling acres
of sunflowers in Spain, mansards
in Vermont, painted shay and pard,

V

or the things I see, driving
with you: houses and cars, trees,
grasses and birds; people, incidents
of the senses—like women and men, dusk

on a golf course, waving clubs
dreamily in slow practice-gestures
profiled against a sky layered
purpleish turquoise and gray, having

sport in the evening; or white
selvage of a mockingbird's gray
blur as he dabbles wings and tail
in a gutter—all in a way fraught,

full of emotion, and yet empty—
how can I say it?—all empty
of sadness and happiness, deep
blank passions, waiting like houses

and cars of a strange place,
a profound emptiness that came once
in the car, your cheekbone, lashes,
hair at my vision's edge, driving

VI

back from Vermont and then
into the iron dusk of Cambridge,
Central Square suddenly become
the most strange of places

as a Salvation Army band marches
down the middle, shouldering aside
the farting, evil-tempered traffic,
brass pitting its triplets and sixteenths

into the sundown fray of cops, gesturing
derelicts, young girls begging quarters,
shoppers and released secretaries, scruffy
workers and students, dropouts, children

whistling, gathering as the band
steps in place tootling and rumbling
in the square now, under an apocalypse
of green-and-pink sky, with paper

and filth spinning in the wind, crazy,
everyone—band, audience, city, lady
trumpeter fiddling spit-valve, John
Philip Sousa, me, Christianity, crazy

VII

and all empty except for you,
who look sometimes like a stranger;
as a favorite room, lake, picture
might look seen after years away,

your face at a new angle grows
unfamiliar and blank, love's face
perhaps, where I chose once to dream
again, but better, those past failures—

"Some lovely, glorious Nothing," Susan,
Patricia, Celia, forgive me—God,
a girl in my street was called Half-
A-Buck, not right in her head . . .

how happy I would be, or else
decently sad, with no past: you
only and no foolish ghosts
urging me to become some redeeming

Jewish-American Shakespeare
(or God knows what they expect,
Longfellow) and so excuse my thorny
egotism, my hard-ons of self-concern,

VIII

melodramas and speeches
of myself, crazy in love with
my status as a sad young man: dreams
of myself old, a vomit-stained

ex-Jazz-Immortal, collapsed
in a phlegmy Bowery doorway
on Old Mr. Boston lemon-flavored
gin or on cheap wine—that romantic

fantasy of my future bumhood
excused all manner of lies, fumbles,
destructions, even this minute, *"Mea
culpa!"* I want to scream, stealing

the podium to address the band,
the kids, the old ladies awaiting
buses, the glazed winos (who accomplished
my dream while I got you, and art,

and daughters): "Oh you city of
undone deathcrotches! Terrible
the film of green brainpus! Fog
of corruption at the great shitfry! No

IX

grease-trickling sink
of disorder in your depressed
avenues is more terrible
than these, and not your whole

aggregate of pollution
is more heavy than the measure
of unplumbed muttering
remorse, shame, inchoate pride

and nostalgia in any one
sulphur-choked, grit-breathing
citizen of the place. . . ." Sad,
the way one in part enjoys

air pollution, relishes
millennial doom, headlines,
even the troubles of friends—
or, OK, enjoys hearing

and talking about them, anyway—
to be whole-hearted is rare;
changing as the heart does, is it
the heart, or the sun emerging from

X

or going behind a cloud,
or a change somewhere in my eyes?
Terrible, to think that mere pretty
scenery—or less, the heraldic shape

of an oak leaf drifting down
curbside waters in the sun, pink
bittersweet among the few last
gray sad leaves of the fall—can bring

joy, or fail to. Shouldn't I vow
to seek only within myself
my only hire? Or not? All my senses,
like beacon's flame, counsel gratitude

for the two bright-faced girls
crossing the Square, beauty a light
or intelligence, no quarters for them,
long legs flashing bravely above

the grime—it is as if men were to
go forth plumed in white
uniforms and swords; how could we
ever aspire to such smartness,

XI

such happy grace? Pretty enough
plumage and all, a man in the bullshit
eloquence of his sad praises stumbles,
fumbles: *fool*. It is true, wonder

does indeed hinder love and hate,
and one can behold well with eyes
only what lies beneath him—
so that it takes more than eyes

to see well anything that is worth
loving; that is the sad part, the senses
are not visionary, they can tug
downward, even in pure joy—

trivial joy, the deep solid crack
of the bat. A sandlot home run
has led me to clown circling
the diamond as though cheered

by a make-believe audience
of thousands (you, dead poets, friends,
old coaches and teachers, everyone
I ever knew) cheering louder as I tip

XII

my imaginary, ironic hat and blow
false kisses crossing home, happiness
impure and oddly memorable as the sad
agony of recalled errors lived over

before sleep, poor throws awry
or the ball streaming through,
between my poor foolish legs, crouching
amazëd like a sot. Sport—woodmanship,

ball games, court games—has its cruel
finitude of skill, good-and-bad, as does
the bizarre art of words: confirmation
of a good word, *polvo*, dust, reddish gray

powder of the ballfield, *el polvo*
rising in pale puffs to glaze lightly
the brown ankles and brown bare feet in
Cervantes' poem of the girl dancing, all

dust now, poet, girl. It is intolerable
to think of my daughters, too, dust—
el polvo—or you whose invented game,
Sadness and Happiness, soothes them

XIII

to sleep: can you tell me one sad
thing that happened today, Can you think
of one happy thing to tell me that
happened to you today, organizing

life—not you too dust like the poets,
dancers, athletes, their dear skills
and the alleged glittering gaiety of
Art which, in my crabwise scribbling hand,

no less than Earth the change of all
changes breedeth, art and life
both inconstant mothers, in whose
fixed cold bosoms we lie fixed,

desperate to devise anything, any
sadness or happiness, only
to escape the clasped coffinworm
truth of eternal art or marmoreal

infinite nature, twin stiff
destined measures both manifested
by my shoes, coated with dust or dew which no
earthly measure will survive.

III. Persons

To My Father

FOR MILFORD S. PINSKY

The glazed surface of the world, dusk
And three mallard that land
In the dim lake, each

Scudding in a bright oval . . .
What chance, man, for the thin
Halting qualities of the soul?

Call this, prologue to an explanation,
Something like the way Uncle Joe Winograd
With a carpenter's flat silence

Might act on some given stretch
Of Uncle Italo Tarantola's lifelong
Lawyerly expanding monologue.

What I wanted, was to dwell
Here in the brain as though
At my bench, as though in a place

Like the live ongoing shop—
Between kitchen and factory—
Of a worker in wood or in leather:

Implements ranged in sizes and shapes,
The stuff itself stacked up
In the localized purposeful clutter

Of work, the place itself smelling
Of the hide, sawdust or whatever.
I wanted the exact words;

I wanted the way to pronounce
Evenly the judgment which a man
Who is quiet holds back as distinct

But not final in the presence
Of a good talker. I a good talker
Ask you a quiet man to recall the inside

Of a shop, glassdust and lenses
Everywhere, broken eyeglasses, forms
And odd pieces of paper, voices

Like phones ringing, tools
Broken and whole everywhere, mail
Unread, the sign—"Milford S." or

"Robert"—hanging like a straight face . . .
Surface, tyranny of the world visible,
Images that spread outward

From the brain like lines crazing—
Or like brief silvery ovals
That glide over the dark,

Ethereal, yet each wingbeat
Firm in time, of more
Substance than this, this mothlike

Stirring of words, work or affection.

Old Woman

Not even in darkest August,
When the mysterious insects
Marry loudly in the black weeds
And the woodbine, limp after rain,
In the cooled night is more fragrant,
Do you gather in any slight
Harvest to yourself. Deep whispers
Of slight thunder, horizons off,
May break your thin sleep, but awake,
You cannot hear them. Harsh gleaner
Of children, grandchildren—remnants
Of nights now forever future—
Your dry, invisible shudder
Dies on this porch where, uninflamed,
You dread the oncoming seasons,
Repose in the electric night.

Library Scene

TO P.M.S.

Under the ceiling of metal stamped like plaster
And below the ceiling fan, in the brown lustre

Someone is reading, in the sleepy room
Alert, her damp cheek balanced on one palm,

With knuckles loosely holding back the pages
Or fingers waiting lightly at their edges.

Her eyes are like the eyes of someone attending
To a fragile work, familiar and demanding—

Some work of delicate surfaces or threads.
Someone is reading the way a rare child reads,

A kind of changeling reading for love of reading,
For love and for the course of something leading

Her child's intelligent soul through its inflection:
A force, a kind of loving work or action.

Someone is reading in a deepening room
Where something happens, something that will come

To happen again, happening as many times
As she is reading in as many rooms.

What happens outside that calm like water braiding
Over green stones? The ones of little reading

Or who never read for love, are many places.
They are in the house of power, and many houses

Reading as they do, doing what they do.
Or it happens that they come, at times, to you

Because you are somehow someone that they need:
They come to you and you tell them how you read.

First Early Mornings Together

Waking up over the candy store together
We hear birds waking up below the sill
And slowly recognize ourselves, the weather,
The time, and the birds that rustle there until

Down to the street as fog and quiet lift
The pigeons from the wrinkled awning flutter
To reconnoiter, mutter, stare and shift
Pecking by ones or twos the rainbowed gutter.

The Sentences

Reading the sentences, November sun
Touching the avenues, offices, the station,
I saw you pass me on a street, your face
Was pink with cold, cold windows flashed, the stores
And cars were like—mythology—, the street
Itself was glamorous and lost, it was
As though I never knew you yet somehow knew
That this was you, a sentence interdicted
The present, it said, *you never knew*, you passed,
Leaves coppery and quick as lizards moved
Around your delicate ankles; November sun
Lay on the sidewalk, ordinary and final
As the sentences too flat for any poem.

Daughter

I

She thinks about skeletons,
Admires their symmetry,
Responding with fear
To the implied movement
And the near-absence of expression.
In the museum
Of natural history
She pressed up close
To the smaller ones;
But shook, studying the tall
Scaffolding of dinosaurs
From the next room.
Back home, sitting in the john
With the door open
She claims to see, in a mirror
Down the dark hall, her own.

II

At certain times, midway
In a meal, or feeling
The dried mucus of her nose
She stares nowhere like a cat.
It is not quite the same
As the damp sensual trance
Of her thumb. It does not
Seem to be thought, nor
The deep stare of a cat
Concentrating on a noise

Or a smell. It is like a cat
Staring nowhere. When she comes
Out of it or is interrupted
A great emptiness flares,
Of profound privacy,
Like a good Christian's death.

III

With people, she deals oddly.
Normally too savage for bribes,
She attaches herself
In the way of a feudal tenant
To a grandma, overweight,
Spendthrift. The vassal
Declares prices,
Then haggles for a while.
She watches the two
Parents as they watch her
Pleasing herself with cheap
Toys and half-eaten sweets.
Chattering as two equals,
Nicole who calls herself "Mary"
And the woman nobody loves enough
Trot downtown for their perms.

IV

Like most children
She paints openly and well,
Somewhat like Henri Rousseau.
She and her friends paint
With a mild firmness
Of attention. Their great
Interest when they discuss
Paintings they have made

Seems partly affected:
A habit, maybe, grown
From the ineluctable
Deal that their kind make.
Is the painting also
Part of the deal? Often, she
Smears over her work, thick
Strokes, as for painting a wall.

V

She chats quietly
With a few cronies
On the subject of death.
They all have something to say,
Her contribution being
To list her close family
In correct order of age,
Declaring that we will die
In the same order. Nobody
Disagrees. *I know it,*
They say, *I know it.* One
Tells about graves. And then
They drift off the subject
Like that many businesslike
Starlings, flying away
From one tree among trees.

The Personal Devil

Ink, fire, quintuple mirrors—
By means bizarre enough,
I convoked the multiple eye
And saw from claw to scruff
The growth that Being nurtured:
The subtle bully whose Days—
His furies and lackeys and bearers—
Hang like the dozing flies
Whose billions in bog or orchard
Gorge with a daylong sigh.

The devices I arrayed
Conjured features like mine,
A familiar shape that I
Denied—denied as the bane
Of myself, the multifarious
Event that pulls my face
To its own. As I watched it fade
I saw myself take place,
Crystalline, in the iris
Of the huge, dissolving eye.

Spelunker

With flecks of web like foam
Still clinging to his brow and back
The deep explorer in his dream
Of rescue turns to seek

The faces of his friends
Already, as his arms come out
Into their cheering hands
Pulling him to the light

(Which thanks to certain drugs
Will not offend his eyes or skin)
And they will all be there; his legs
Will still be dangling down

Into the simple depth
(No symbol, no Womb or Self or Grave,
Neither his birth nor death
But a confusing cave

Where he is hurt and lost),
His feet still hanging in the dark
When to his mouth which they have kissed
The friends will hold a drink

Miraculously bright and cool,
The elixir of his dream,
His dream which marks the pall
Of darkness with cool stars for him,

Hallucinations which he knows
Are common in his plight
And which he now construes
As will-to-live, a faith in light

Surviving, so that he has come
To welcome this false Zodiac
Because it is his dream
Of rescue: for the sake

Of untrue lights to climb
Or burrow the expanding darkness
Which also is his dream
Of rescue, or the dream's dark likeness.

The Generation Before

TO FRANK BIDART

The wind blew. Some days, rain
Falling the size of nickels
Splashed up over the curb.
There were hats for that, and for sun
Too, frying shoeleather in its hot cycles.
Flesh was a poor garb,

So poor, the people were quaint—
Muffled up into their high cars
Or their quaint bulky clothing.
In the prolonged slap-happy Lent
Of the times, harder than yours,
Eating or asleep, breathing,

They got by in their manner, at times
Made Carnival in hotel bars,
At ball games or the track. In photographs,
In films, even in their haberdashery, games
And swank gear (cases, lighters,
Syphons, clips, objects for looks or laughs

Of glass, pigskin, malachite)
They survive as a vague murmur of style,
The nostalgic false life of a face
Shining from a snapshot. Time will not
Light gently on those fathers. They will fall
Sick in the lungs and the heart, hapless

In a motel, swearing at their own lost
Flickery past, craving a field
Empty and large, the growth pale and recent
Over the plow-twisting tangle of the past—
The grasses coarse, unculled,
The impossible field of the present.

44

IV. The Street Of Furthest Memory

The Street Of Furthest Memory

The street flails
old substances, a chaff
of felt, beaver-board,

slate shingles, tarpaper—plain
or made to resemble masonry
and brick—, oilcloth, sharkskin.

In a film of rain, the street
shines. Luncheonette,
lot, shoemaker,

They get clearer
in the rain, a spring rain
patched with sun,

the bright drops on glass,
on awnings of canvas, on cars
moving down the street

as the awnings flap,
flickering like a torn
film, coupe and sedan passing

to beyond your earliest
memory, on the street
out of memory, the sweet

street flailing its
lost substances, tangling
off as though thrown

from the spinning black
reel, unthreading rapidly, like
panic flailing the street.

Long Branch, New Jersey

Everything is regional,
And this is where I was born, dear,
And conceived,
And first moved to tears,
And last irritated to the same point.

It is bounded on three sides by similar places
And on one side by vast, uncouth houses
A glum boardwalk and,
As we say, The Beach.

I stand here now
At the corner of Third Avenue and Broadway
Waiting for you to come by in a car,
And count the red carlights
That rush through a fine rain
To where Broadway's two branches—North
Broadway and South Broadway—both reach
To the trite, salt, welcoming ocean.

Doctor Frolic

Felicity the healer isn't young
And you don't look him up unless you need him.
Clown's eyes, Pope's nose, a mouth for dirty stories,
He made his bundle in the Great Depression

And now, a jovial immigrant success
In baggy pinstripes, he winks and wheezes gossip,
Village stories that could lift your hair
Or lance a boil; the small town dirt, the dope,

The fishy deals and incestuous combinations,
The husband and the wife of his wife's brother,
The hospital contract, the certificate . . .
A realist and hardy omnivore,

He strolls the jetties when the month is right
With a knife and lemons in his pocket, after
Live mussels from among the smelly rocks,
Preventative of impotence and goitre.

And as though the sight of tissue healing crooked
Pleased him, like the ocean's vaginal taste,
He'll stitch your thumb up so it shows for life.
And where he once was the only quack in town

We all have heard his half-lame joke, the one
About the operation that succeeded,
The tangy line that keeps that clever eye
So merry in the punchinello face.

Pleasure Pier

With noises meaningful and vague as ever
The surf goes through its motions of attack.
Black water foams and comes erect and charges
White up the dark beach and collapses back to black.

Black under my feet, it sucks the kelp-haired pilings
That hold Convention Hall's Venetian folly
Up over the waters. The November air,
The boardwalk's void perspective, the melancholy

Of minarets and blistered stucco are blatant,
Crude as my crude vague needs, old hopes that dwell
On a violent urgency of color—blue mane
Of a horse frozen on the carousel,

A shooting-gallery bear whose eyes glare purple.
Among the sleeping pinballs and arcades
My boyhood lurks, as the phantom from a film
That the locale helps me dream. Hot-eyed, he wades

The boatride's oily channel, sleeps curled up
Among gears and pipes like viscera. In his arms
As he hurries through the tunnels of the Fun House
Is the Girl, the virgin whom he never harms.

Saved, she can't look when in the final scene
He dies in flames that throw their stagey lights
Out onto the water, the weary muttering waves
That pulled and worried at his prison's roots.

The Destruction Of Long Branch

When they came out with artificial turf
I went back home with a thousand miles.

I dug a trench by moonlight from the ocean
And let it wash in quietly

And make a brackish quicksand which the tide
Sluiced upward from the streets and ditches.

The downtown that the shopping centers killed,
The garden apartments, the garages,

The station, the Little Africa on (so help me)
Liberty Street, the nicer sections,

All settled gently in a drench of sand
And sunk with a minimum of noise.

The hollow of the shut-down movie house
Made bubbles. Wooden porches crumbled

But ranch homes in the new developments,
Tilting a little, slipped in whole.

I pushed back pieces that floated up: one gash
Of neon, the martini glass

That winked outside a mafia hotel;
A gas pump; a bouquet of socks

From Woolley's window (I even kept a few);
The pinball from my grandpa's bar.

I laid out hills and ridges, and with a brush
I creosoted lumps of sewage

Where the school had shat its plumbing as it went.
I fitted my carpet on the crust

(That made-in-Japan grass went on like magic)
With a neat margin at the beach,

And I still had half the night. "How great," I said . . .
Then, since forgiving had been fun

I thought I'd leave a monument or two.
Cautiously elegiac, I dug

Some scenes back up to compose my parkland vistas:
Benches and gloomy vegetation,

Some things already dead, an abandoned boardwalk,
Some weather, an unfilled foundation—

With a brush of huckleberry or a ragged fern,
Cabbagey growth along a curb,

Thin flags of sumac from a vacant lot
Avid in a tearing rain.

The Beach Women

In the fierce peak of the day it's quietly they wade
With spread arms into the blue breakers rushing white
And swim seemingly with no tension, the arms
Curved, the head's gestures circular and slow.

They walk dripping back into the air
Of nineteen-fifty-five smiling downward from the glare
As if modestly, as they move daintily over the sand
Shaking their hair, tingling, taking it easy.

The beach flushes and broils, shapes ripple
In the waves of heat over it and the cold sea-water
Dries on their arms and legs and their suits, too,
Drying out stretched over their bottoms

In the luxury of sun flowering everywhere. The delicate
Salt glazing their skin they dissolve in oil.
Holiday colors throb on suits, towels, blankets,
Footwear, loose robes, bottles, carriers of straw,

Bright magazines and books, gear feminine and abundant
The whole overwhelming with a sense less of sex than
    gender,
The great oval blanks of their sunglasses hypnotic,
Flashing anonymous glamour over their cards, books or
    gossip.

It was Irving Stone they read, John O'Hara or
    Herman Wouk
Or the decade's muse of adultery: Grace Metalious.
With her picture in *Time*, floppy dungarees, no bra,
Retrospectively a seer, a social critic—

No doubt the cabana-boys weren't always lying
About their own ladies, mistresses whose husbands
Came down from New York to tip big on the week-end—
Like Mrs. F, strawberry-blond Italian . . .

What did she carry down to the sand all summer
But Wouk's *Caine Mutiny*, the earnest young sailors
Behaving like so many Jews, coming over guilty
Because they hadn't let Hitler as Lloyd Nolan

Played by Joe McCarthy send them under the waves.
Good for Grace, writing about "lust" with her flat
Characters and her big breasts. What did Mrs. F
Sunning at the shore fifteen years ago, or anyone,

Think about Caryl Chessman, Chaplin, Lucky Luciano,
Ike and the Rosenbergs? What can I recall? Women,
Moving in the sparkle of the sidewalk, blinding
Even in the reverse colors of the afterimage

Outside the drugstore where I worked, no cabana Lancelot,
Grateful for a wet cuddle with a chubby majorette.
I made club sandwiches and sundaes, on dark days purveyed
Dozens of copies of *Confidential*: "Victor Mature

Locked Me In A Cage" and "Russ Tamblyn's All Girl
    Party"
Cheered them up while the rain slashed gray
Soaking the boardwalk and gleaming on cars.
On those days I admired their tans, white dresses,

And pink oval fingernails on brown hands, and sold them
Perfume and lipstick, aspirins, throat lozenges and Tums,
Tampax, newspapers and paperback books—brave stays
Against boredom, discomfort, death and old age.

V. Essay On Psychiatrists

Essay On Psychiatrists

I. Invocation

It's crazy to think one could describe them—
Calling on reason, fantasy, memory, eyes and ears—
As though they were all alike any more

Than sweeps, opticians, poets or masseurs.
Moreover, they are for more than one reason
Difficult to speak of seriously and freely,

And I have never (even this is difficult to say
Plainly, without foolishness or irony)
Consulted one for professional help, though it happens

Many or most of my friends have—and that,
Perhaps, is why it seems urgent to try to speak
Sensibly about them, about the psychiatrists.

II. Some Terms

"Shrink" is a misnomer. The religious
Analogy is all wrong, too, and the old,
Half-forgotten jokes about Viennese accents

And beards hardly apply to the good-looking woman
In boots and a knit dress, or the man
Seen buying the Sunday *Times* in mutton-chop

Whiskers and expensive jogging shoes.
In a way I suspect that even the terms "doctor"
And "therapist" are misnomers; the patient

Is not necessarily "sick." And one assumes
That no small part of the psychiatrist's
Role is just that: to point out misnomers.

III. Proposition

These are the first citizens of contingency.
Far from the doctrinaire past of the old ones,
They think in their prudent meditations

Not about ecstasy (the soul leaving the body)
Nor enthusiasm (the god entering one's person)
Nor even about sanity (which means

Health, an impossible perfection)
But ponder instead relative truth and the warm
Dusk of amelioration. The cautious

Young augurs with their family-life, good books
And records and foreign cars believe
In amelioration—in that, and in suffering.

IV. A Lakeside Identification

Yes, crazy to suppose one could describe them—
And yet, there was this incident: at the local beach
Clouds of professors and the husbands of professors

Swam, dabbled or stood to talk with arms folded
Gazing at the lake . . . and one of the few townsfolk there,
With no faculty status—a matter-of-fact, competent,

Catholic woman of twenty-seven with five children
And a first-rate body—pointed her finger
At the back of one certain man and asked me,

"Is that guy a psychiatrist?" and by god he was! "Yes,"
She said, "He *looks* like a psychiatrist."
Grown quiet, I looked at his pink back, and thought.

V. Physical Comparison With Professors And Others

Pink and a bit soft-bodied, with a somewhat jazzy
Middle-class bathing suit and sandy sideburns, to me
He looked from the back like one more professor.

And from the front, too—the boyish, unformed carriage
Which foreigners always note in American men, combined
As in a professor with that liberal, quizzical,

Articulate gaze so unlike the more focused, more
Tolerant expression worn by a man of action (surgeon,
Salesman, athlete). On closer inspection was there,

Perhaps, a self-satisfied or benign air, a studied
Gentleness toward the child whose hand he held loosely?
Absurd to speculate; but then—the woman saw *something*.

> VI. Their Seriousness, With Further
>   Comparisons

In a certain sense, they are not serious.
That is, they are serious—useful, deeply helpful,
Concerned—only in the way that the pilots of huge

Planes, radiologists, and master mechanics can,
At their best, be serious. But however profound
The psychiatrists may be, they are not serious the way

A painter may be serious beyond pictures, or a businessman
May be serious beyond property and cash—or even
The way scholars and surgeons are serious, each rapt

In his work's final cause, contingent upon nothing:
Beyond work; persons; recoveries. And this is fitting:
Who would want to fly with a pilot who was *serious*

About getting to the destination safely? Terrifying idea—
That a pilot could over-extend, perhaps try to fly
Too well, or suffer from Pilot's Block; of course,

It may be that (just as they must not drink liquor
Before a flight) they undergo regular, required check-ups
With a psychiatrist, to prevent such things from happening.

VII. Historical (*The Bacchae*)

Madness itself, as an idea, leaves us confused—
Incredulous that it exists, or cruelly facetious,
Or stricken with a superstitious awe as if bound

By the lost cults of Trebizond and Pergamum . . .
The most profound study of madness is found
In the *Bacchae* of Euripides, so deeply disturbing

That in Cambridge, Massachusetts the players
Evaded some of the strongest unsettling material
By portraying poor sincere, fuddled, decent Pentheus

As a sort of fascistic bureaucrat—but it is Dionysus
Who holds rallies, instills exaltations of violence,
With his leopards and atavistic troops above law,

Reason and the good sense and reflective dignity
Of Pentheus—Pentheus, humiliated, addled, made to suffer
Atrocity as a minor jest of the smirking God.

When Bacchus's Chorus (who call him "most gentle"!)
    observe:
"Ten thousand men have ten thousand hopes; some fail,
Some come to fruit, but the happiest man is he

Who gathers the good of life day by day"—as though
Life itself were enough—does that mean, to leave ambition?
And is it a kind of therapy, or truth? Or both?

VIII. A Question

On the subject of madness the *Bacchae* seems,
On the whole, more *pro* than *contra*. The Chorus
Says of wine, "There is no other medicine for misery";

When the Queen in her ecstasy—or her enthusiasm?—
Tears her terrified son's arm from his body, or bears
His head on her spear, she remains happy so long

As she remains crazy; the God himself (who bound fawnskin
To the women's flesh, armed them with ivy arrows
And his orgies' livery) debases poor Pentheus first,

Then leads him to mince capering towards female Death
And dismemberment: flushed, grinning, the grave young
King of Thebes pulls at a slipping bra-strap, simpers

Down at his turned ankle. *Pentheus*: "Should I lift up
Mount Cithæron—Bacchae, mother and all?"
Dionysus: "Do what you want to do. Your mind

Was unstable once, but now you sound more sane,
You are on your way to great things." The question is,
Which is the psychiatrist: Pentheus, or Dionysus?

IX. Pentheus As Psychiatrist

With his reasonable questions Pentheus tries
To throw light on the old customs of savagery.
Like a brave doctor, he asks about it all,

He hears everything, "Weird, fantastic things"
The Messenger calls them: with their breasts
Swollen, their new babies abandoned, mothers

Among the Bacchantes nestled gazelles
And young wolves in their arms, and suckled them;
You might see a single one of them tear a fat calf

In two, still bellowing with fright, while others
Clawed heifers to pieces; ribs and hooves
Were strewn everywhere; blood-smeared scraps

Hung from the fir trees; furious bulls
Charged and then fell stumbling, pulled down
To be stripped of skin and flesh by screaming women . . .

And Pentheus listened. Flames burned in their hair,
Unnoticed; thick honey spurted from their wands;
And the snakes they wore like ribbons licked

Hot blood from their flushed necks: Pentheus
Was the man the people told . . . "weird things," like
A middle-class fantasy of release; and when even

The old men—bent Cadmus and Tiresias—dress up
In fawnskin and ivy, beating their wands on the ground,
Trying to carouse, it is Pentheus—down-to-earth,

Sober—who raises his voice in the name of dignity.
Being a psychiatrist, how could he attend to the Chorus's
    warning
Against "those who aspire" and "a tongue without reins"?

X. Dionysus As Psychiatrist

In a more hostile view, the psychiatrists
Are like Bacchus—the knowing smirk of his mask,
His patients, his confident guidance of passion,

And even his little jokes, as when the great palace
Is hit by lightning which blazes and stays,
Bouncing among the crumpling stone walls . . .

And through the burning rubble he comes,
With his soft ways picking along lightly
With a calm smile for the trembling Chorus

Who have fallen to the ground, bowing
In the un-Greek, Eastern way—What, Asian women,
He asks, Were you disturbed just now when Bacchus

Jostled the palace? He warns Pentheus to adjust,
To learn the ordinary man's humble sense of limits,
Violent limits, to the rational world. He cures

Pentheus of the grand delusion that the dark
Urgencies can be governed simply by the mind,
And the mind's will. He teaches Queen Agave to look

Up from her loom, up at the light, at her tall
Son's head impaled on the stiff spear clutched
In her own hand soiled with dirt and blood.

XI. Their Philistinism Considered

"Greek Tragedy" of course is the sort of thing
They like and like the idea of . . . though not "tragedy"
In the sense of newspapers. When a patient shot one of
    them,

People phoned in, many upset as though a deep,
Special rule had been abrogated, someone had gone too far.
The poor doctor, as described by the evening *Globe*,

Turned out to be a decent, conventional man (Doctors
For Peace, B'Nai Brith, numerous articles), almost
Carefully so, like Paul Valéry—or like Rex Morgan, M.D.,
    who,

In the same *Globe*, attends a concert with a longjawed
    woman.
First Panel: *"We're a little early for the concert!*
There's an art museum we can stroll through!" "I'd like

That, Dr. Morgan!" Second Panel: *"Outside the hospital,*
There's no need for such formality, Karen! Call me
By my first name!" "I'll feel a little awkward!"

Final Panel: *"Meanwhile . . ."* a black car pulls up
To City Hospital. . . . By the next day's *Globe*, the real
Doctor has died of gunshot wounds, while for smiling,
    wooden,

Masklike Rex and his companion the concert has passed,
Painlessly, offstage: *"This was a beautiful experience,*
   Rex!"
"I'm glad you enjoyed it! I have season tickets

And you're welcome to use them! I don't have
The opportunity to go to many of the concerts!"
Second Panel: *"You must be famished!"* And so Rex

And Karen go off to smile over a meal which will pass
Like music offstage, off to the mysterious pathos
Of their exclamation-marks, while in the final panel

"Meanwhile, In The Lobby At City Hospital"
A longjawed man paces furiously among
The lamps, magazines, tables and tubular chairs.

XII. Their Philistinism Dismissed

But after all—what "cultural life" and what
Furniture, what set of the face, would seem adequate
For those who supply medicine for misery?

After all, what they do is in a way a kind of art,
And what writers have to say about music, or painters'
Views about poetry, musicians' taste in pictures, all

Often are similarly hoked-up, dutiful, vulgar. After all,
They are not gods or heroes, nor even priests chosen
Apart from their own powers, but like artists are mere

Experts dependent on their own wisdom, their own arts:
Pilgrims in the world, journeymen, bourgeois savants,
Gallant seekers and persistent sons, doomed

To their cruel furniture and their season tickets
As to skimped meditations and waxen odes.
At first, Rex Morgan seems a perfect Pentheus—

But he smirks, he is imperturbable, he understates;
Understatement is the privilege of a god, we must
Choose, we must find out which way to see them:

Either the bland arrogance of the abrupt mountain god
Or the man of the town doing his best, we must not
Complain both that they are inhuman and too human.

XIII. Their Despair

I am quite sure that I have read somewhere
That the rate of suicide among psychiatrists
Is far higher than for any other profession.

There are many myths to explain such things, things
Which one reads and believes without believing
Any one significance for them—as in this case,

Which again reminds me of writers, who, I have read,
Drink and become alcoholics and die of alcoholism
In far greater numbers than other people.

Symmetry suggests one myth, or significance: the drinking
Of writers coming from too much concentration,
In solitude, upon feelings expressed

For or even about possibly indifferent people, people
Who are absent or perhaps dead, or unborn; the suicide
Of psychiatrists coming from too much attention,

In most intimate contact, concentrated upon the feelings
Of people toward whom one may feel indifferent,
People who are certain, sooner or later, to die . . .

Or people about whom they care too much, after all?
The significance of any life, of its misery and its end,
Is not absolute—that is the despair which

Underlies their good sense, recycling their garbage,
Voting, attending town-meetings, synagogues, churches,
Weddings, contingent gatherings of all kinds.

XIV. Their Speech, Compared With Wisdom And Poetry

Terms of all kinds mellow with time, growing
Arbitrary and rich as we call this man "neurotic"
Or that man "a peacock." The lore of psychiatrists—

"Paranoid," "Anal" and so on, if they still use
Such terms—also passes into the status of old sayings:
Water thinner than blood or under bridges; bridges

Crossed in the future or burnt in the past. Or the terms
Of myth, the phrases that well up in my mind:
Two blind women and a blind little boy, running—

Easier to cut thin air into planks with a saw
And then drive nails into those planks of air,
Than to evade those three, the blind harriers,

The tireless blind women and the blind boy, pursuing
For long years of my life, for long centuries of time.
Concerning Justice, Fortune and Love I believe

That there may be wisdom, but no science and few terms:
Blind, and blinding, too. Hot in pursuit and flight,
Justice, Fortune and Love demand the arts

Of knowing and naming: and, yes, the psychiatrists, too,
Patiently naming them. But all in pursuit and flight, two
Blind women, tireless, and the blind little boy.

XV. A Footnote Concerning Psychiatry Itself

Having mentioned it, though it is not
My subject here, I will say only that one
Hopes it is good, and hopes that practicing it

The psychiatrists who are my subject here
Will respect the means, however pathetic,
That precede them; that they respect the patient's

Own previous efforts, strategies, civilizations—
Not only whatever it is that lets a man consciously
Desire girls of sixteen (or less) on the street,

And not embrace them, et cetera, but everything that was
There already: the restraints, and the other lawful
Old culture of wine, women, et cetera.

XVI. Generalizing, Just And Unjust

As far as one can generalize, only a few
Are not Jewish. Many, I have heard, grew up
As an only child. Among many general charges

Brought against them (smugness, obfuscation)
Is a hard, venal quality. In truth, they do differ
From most people in the special, tax-deductible status

Of their services, an enviable privilege which brings
Venality to the eye of the beholder, who feels
With some justice that if to soothe misery

Is a tax-deductible medical cost, then the lute-player,
Waitress, and actor also deserve to offer
Their services as tax-deductible; movies and TV

Should be tax-deductible . . . or nothing should;
Such cash matters perhaps lead psychiatrists
And others to buy what ought not to be sold: Seder

Services at hotels; skill at games from paid lessons;
Fast divorce; the winning side in a war seen
On TV like cowboys or football—*that* is how much

One can generalize: psychiatrists are as alike (and unlike)
As cowboys. In fact, they are stock characters like cowboys:
"Bette Davis, Claude Rains in *Now Voyager* (1942),

A sheltered spinster is brought out of her shell
By her psychiatrist" and "Steven Boyd, Jack Hawkins
In *The Third Secret* (1964), a psychoanalyst's

Daughter asks a patient to help her find her father's
Murderer." Like a cowboy, the only child roams
The lonely ranges and secret mesas of his genre.

XVII. Their Patients

As a rule, the patients I know do not pace
Furiously, nor scream, nor shoot doctors. For them,
To be a patient seems not altogether different

From one's interest in Anne Landers and her clients:
Her virtue of taking it all on, answering
Any question (artificial insemination by grandpa;

The barracuda of a girl who says that your glasses
Make you look square) and her virtue of saying,
Buster (or Dearie) stop complaining and do

What you want . . . and often that seems to be the point:
After the glassware from Design Research, after
A place on the Cape with Marimekko drapes,

The superlative radio and shoes, comes
The contingency tax—serious people, their capacity
For mere hedonism fills up, one seems to need

To perfect more complex ideas of desire,
To overcome altruism in the technical sense,
To learn to say no when you mean no and yes

When you mean yes, a standard of *cui bono*, a standard
Which, though it seems to be the inverse
Of more Spartan or Christian codes, is no less

Demanding in its call, inward in this case, to duty.
It suggests a kind of league of men and women dedicated
To their separate, inward duties, holding in common

Only the most general standard, or no standard
Other than valuing a sense of the conflict
Among standards, a league recalling in its mutual

Conflict and comfort the well-known fact that psychiatrists,
Too, are the patients of other psychiatrists,
Working dutifully—*cui bono*—at the inward standards.

XVIII. The Mad

Other patients are ill otherwise, and do
Scream and pace and kill or worse; and that
Should be recalled. Kit Smart, Hitler,

The contemporary poets of lunacy—none of them
Helps me to think of the mad otherwise
Than in cliches too broad, the maenads

And wild-eyed killers of the movies . . .
But perhaps lunacy feels something like a cliche,
A desperate or sweet yielding to some broad,

Mechanical simplification, a dispersal
Of the unbearable into its crude fragments,
The distraction of a repeated gesture

Or a compulsively hummed tune. Maybe
It is not utterly different from chewing
At one's fingernails. For the psychiatrists

It must come to seem ordinary, its causes
And the causes of its relief, after all,
No matter how remote and intricate, are no

Stranger than life itself, which was born or caused
Itself, once, as a kind of odor, a faint wreath
Brewing where the radiant light from billions

Of miles off strikes a faint broth from water
Standing in rock; life born from the egg
Of rock, and the egglike rock of death

Are no more strange than this other life
Which we name after the moon, lunatic
Other-life . . . housed, for the lucky ones,

In McLean's Hospital with its elegant,
Prep-school atmosphere. When my friend
Went in, we both tried to joke: "Karen," I said,

"You must be crazy to spend money and time
In this place"—she gained weight,
Made a chess-board, had a room-mate

Who introduced herself as the Virgin Mary,
Referred to another patient: "Well, she must
Be an interesting person, if she's in here."

XIX. Peroration, Defining Happiness

"I know not how it is, but certainly I
Have never been more tired with any reading
Than with dissertations upon happiness,

Which seems not only to elude inquiry,
But to cast unmerciful loads of clay
And sand and husks and stubble

Along the high-road of the inquirer.
Even sound writers talk mostly in a drawling
And dreaming way about it. He,

Who hath given the best definition
Of most things, hath given but an imperfect one,
Here, informing us that a happy life

Is one without impediment to virtue. . . .
In fact, hardly anything which we receive
For truth is really and entirely so,

Let it appear plain as it may, and let
Its appeal be not only to the understanding,
But to the senses; for our words do not follow

The senses exactly; and it is by words
We receive truth and express it."
So says Walter Savage Landor in his Imaginary

Conversation between Sir Philip Sidney
And Fulke Greville, Lord Brooke, all three,
In a sense, my own psychiatrists, shrinking

The sense of contingency and confusion
Itself to a few terms I can quote, ponder
Or type: the idea of wisdom, itself, shrinks.

XX. Peroration, Concerning Genius

As to my own concerns, it seems odd, given
The ideas many of us have about art,
That so many writers, makers of films,

Artists, all suitors of excellence and their own
Genius, should consult psychiatrists, willing
To risk that the doctor in curing

71

The sickness should smooth away the cicatrice
Of genius, too. But it is all bosh, the false
Link between genius and sickness,

Except perhaps as they were linked
By the Old Man, addressing his class
On the first day: "*I know why you are here.*

*You are here to laugh. You have heard of a crazy
Old man who believes that Robert Bridges
Was a good poet; who believes that Fulke*

*Greville was a great poet, greater than Philip
Sidney; who believes that Shakespeare's* Sonnets
Are not all that they are cracked up to be.... Well,

*I will tell you something: I will tell you
What this course is about. Sometime in the middle
Of the Eighteenth Century, along with the rise*

*Of capitalism and scientific method, the logical
Foundations of Western thought decayed and fell apart.
When they fell apart, poets were left*

*With emotions and experiences, and with no way
To examine them. At this time, poets and men
Of genius began to go mad. Gray went mad. Collins*

*Went mad. Kit Smart was mad. William Blake surely
Was a madman. Coleridge was a drug addict, with severe
Depression. My friend Hart Crane died mad. My friend*

*Ezra Pound is mad. But you will not go mad; you will
    grow up
To become happy, sentimental old college professors,
Because they were men of genius, and you*

Are not; and the ideas which were vital
To them are mere amusement to you. I will not
Go mad, because I have understood those ideas...."

He drank wine and smoked his pipe more than he should;
In the end his doctors in order to prolong life
Were forced to cut away most of his tongue.

That was their business. As far as he was concerned
Suffering was life's penalty; wisdom armed one
Against madness; speech was temporary; poetry was truth.

XXI. Conclusion

Essaying to distinguish these men and women,
Who try to give medicine for misery,
From the rest of us, I find I have failed

To discover what essential statement could be made
About psychiatrists that would not apply
To all human beings, or what statement

About all human beings would not apply
Equally to psychiatrists. They, too,
Consult psychiatrists. They try tentatively

To understand, to find healing speech. They work
For truth and for money. They are contingent . . .
They talk and talk . . . they are, in the words

Of a lute-player I met once who despised them,
"Into machines" . . . all true of all, so that it seems
That "psychiatrist" is a synonym for "human being,"

Even in their prosperity which is perhaps
Like their contingency merely more vivid than that
Of lutanists, opticians, poets—all into

Truth, into music, into yearning, suffering,
Into elegant machines and luxuries, with caroling
And kisses, with soft rich cloth and polished

Substances, with cash, tennis and fine electronics,
Liberty of lush and reverend places—goods
And money in their contingency and spiritual

Grace evoke the way we are all psychiatrists,
All fumbling at so many millions of miles
Per minute and so many dollars per hour

Through the exploding or collapsing spaces
Between stars, saying what we can.